Remarkable Reptiles

JAKE WILLIAMS

STERLING CHILDREN'S BOOKS
New York

I'd like to say a special thank you to Harley Price-Davis, Mel Brown, and Phil Trenerry for all their help and support.

—JAKE WILLIAMS

STERLING CHILDREN'S BOOKS
New York

An Imprint of Sterling Publishing Co., Inc.
1166 Avenue of the Americas
New York, NY 10036

Text and illustrations © 2018 Jake Williams
Scientific Advisor: Dr Daniel Pincheira-Donoso

ISBN 978-1-4549-3296-3

Distributed in Canada by Sterling Publishing
c/o Canadian Manda Group, 664 Annette Street
Toronto, Ontario M6S 2C8, Canada

For information about custom editions, special sales, and premium and corporate purchases, please contact Sterling Special Sales at 800-805-5489 or specialsales@sterlingpublishing.com.

Manufactured in China

Lot #:
2 4 6 8 10 9 7 5 3 1

09/18

sterlingpublishing.com

Contents

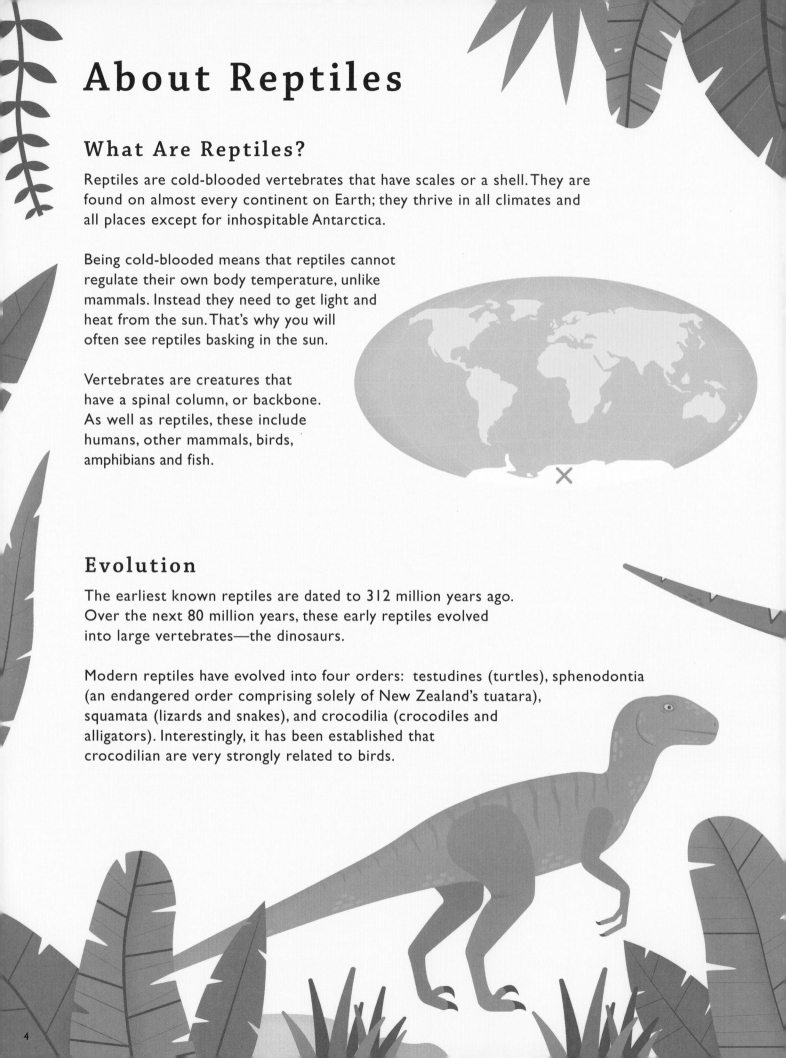

About Reptiles

What Are Reptiles?

Reptiles are cold-blooded vertebrates that have scales or a shell. They are found on almost every continent on Earth; they thrive in all climates and all places except for inhospitable Antarctica.

Being cold-blooded means that reptiles cannot regulate their own body temperature, unlike mammals. Instead they need to get light and heat from the sun. That's why you will often see reptiles basking in the sun.

Vertebrates are creatures that have a spinal column, or backbone. As well as reptiles, these include humans, other mammals, birds, amphibians and fish.

Evolution

The earliest known reptiles are dated to 312 million years ago. Over the next 80 million years, these early reptiles evolved into large vertebrates—the dinosaurs.

Modern reptiles have evolved into four orders: testudines (turtles), sphenodontia (an endangered order comprising solely of New Zealand's tuatara), squamata (lizards and snakes), and crocodilia (crocodiles and alligators). Interestingly, it has been established that crocodilian are very strongly related to birds.

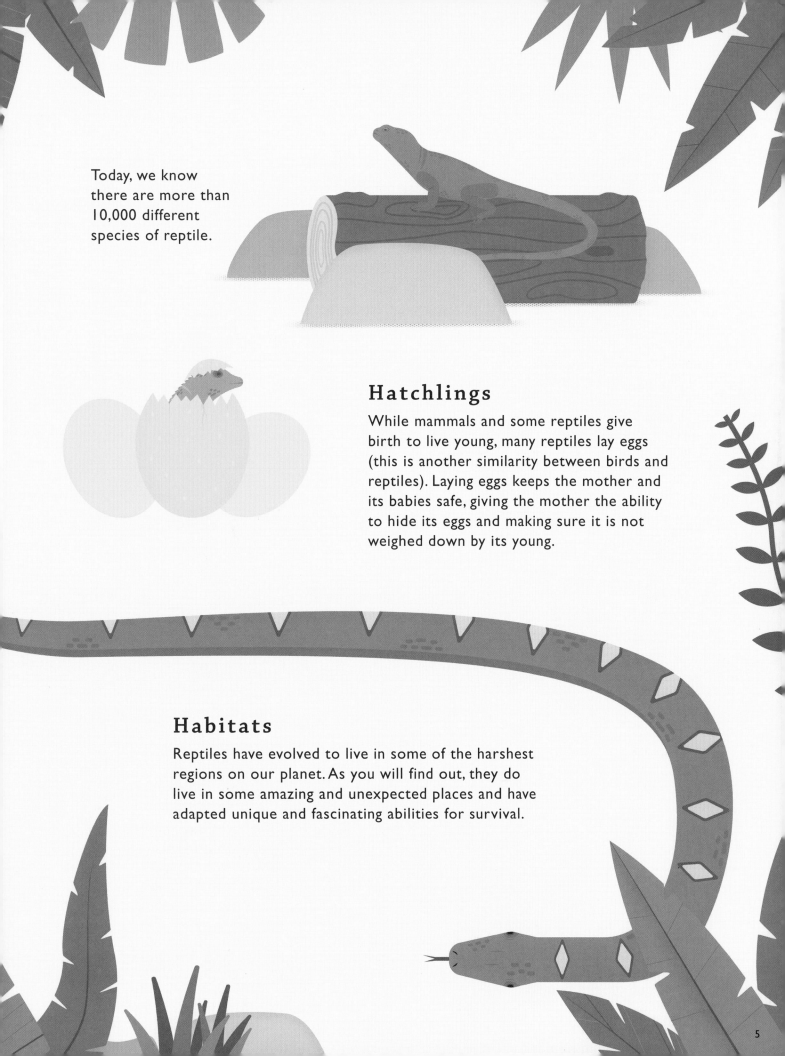

Today, we know there are more than 10,000 different species of reptile.

Hatchlings

While mammals and some reptiles give birth to live young, many reptiles lay eggs (this is another similarity between birds and reptiles). Laying eggs keeps the mother and its babies safe, giving the mother the ability to hide its eggs and making sure it is not weighed down by its young.

Habitats

Reptiles have evolved to live in some of the harshest regions on our planet. As you will find out, they do live in some amazing and unexpected places and have adapted unique and fascinating abilities for survival.

Reptile Timeline

It is well known that reptiles have been around since the age of the dinosaurs. However, it may surprise you to learn that they are even older. They have survived mass extinctions, climate change, and a range of fellow species to evolve into what they have become today.

Turn Back Time

The origins of the reptile go back to about 312 million years ago. To put this in perspective, modern-day humans have only been around for 200,000 years.

Hylonomus

Hylonomus is currently believed to have been the first undeniable reptile. This lizardlike creature walked the earth 312 million years ago—that's nearly 100 million years before the dinosaurs.

Crocodiles

About 215 million years ago, the first true crocodile emerged. Today's crocodiles remain almost unchanged, a testament to how well adapted these animals are to their environments.

Are Birds Reptiles?

Confusingly, although birds aren't reptiles, they are modern dinosaurs. The mass extinction that took place about 65 million years ago wiped out all dinosaurs except for a small group—small, feathered dinosaurs. These survivors evolved over the following 65 million years to become modern-day birds.

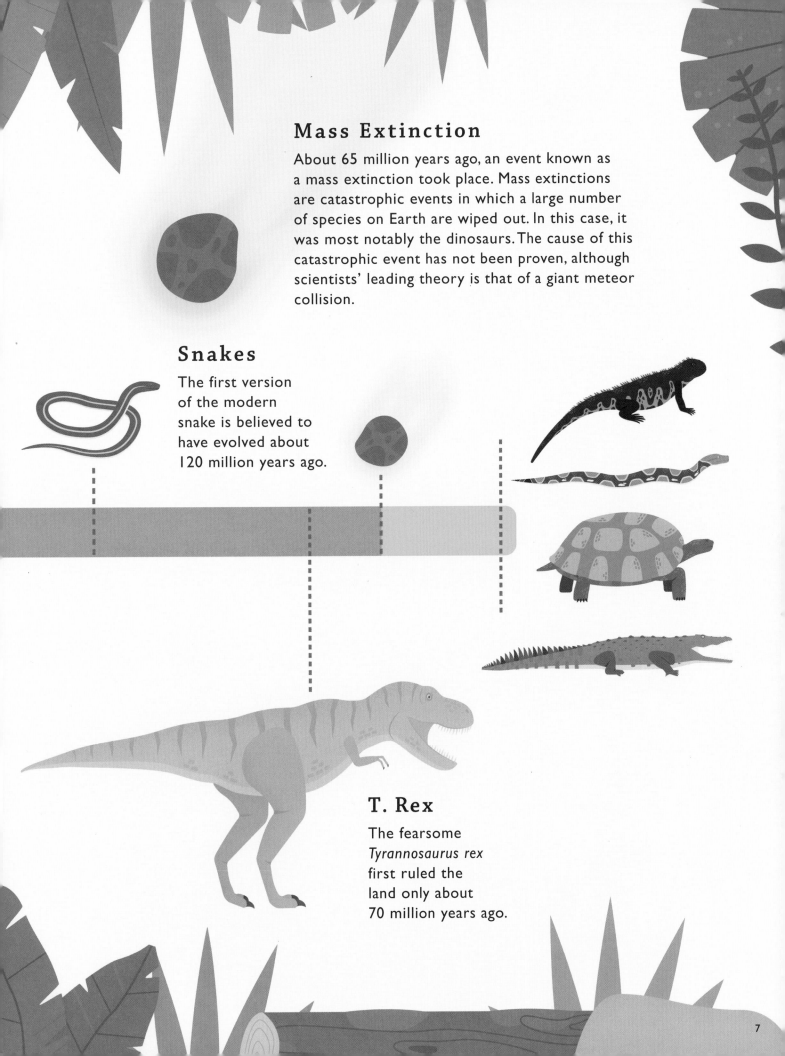

Mass Extinction

About 65 million years ago, an event known as a mass extinction took place. Mass extinctions are catastrophic events in which a large number of species on Earth are wiped out. In this case, it was most notably the dinosaurs. The cause of this catastrophic event has not been proven, although scientists' leading theory is that of a giant meteor collision.

Snakes

The first version of the modern snake is believed to have evolved about 120 million years ago.

T. Rex

The fearsome *Tyrannosaurus rex* first ruled the land only about 70 million years ago.

Reptile Life Cycle

A reptile's life cycle will vary from species to species, however, most species do follow a pattern. As an example, on these pages we will follow the lifecycle of a western skink, from hatching to laying eggs.

1. Juvenile

Like many reptiles, the western skink's life starts as an embryo inside an egg. Reptilian eggs don't tend to be hard, like a chicken's egg, but are instead made out of a leathery material that can expand with the growing embryo. A small number of reptiles can give birth to live young, just like mammals.

2. Hatchling

When the embryo is ready to hatch, it uses a tiny notch on the front of its head to help break through the shell. This is known as an egg tooth.

3. Infant

Unlike a human infant, the newly hatched reptile is completely capable of looking after itself from birth. Because young reptiles are easy targets for predators (sometimes even adults of their own species), they hatch with an excellent understanding of danger (and how to avoid it). Some lizards will even hatch early if they sense the vibrations of a potential predator.

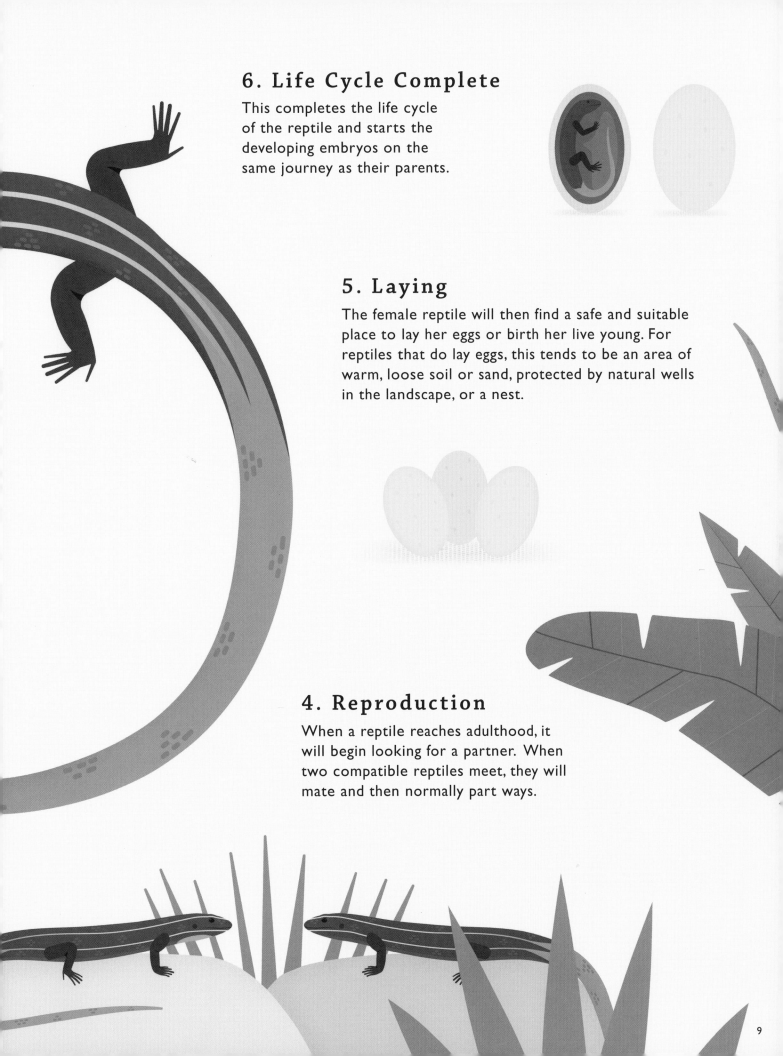

6. Life Cycle Complete

This completes the life cycle of the reptile and starts the developing embryos on the same journey as their parents.

5. Laying

The female reptile will then find a safe and suitable place to lay her eggs or birth her live young. For reptiles that do lay eggs, this tends to be an area of warm, loose soil or sand, protected by natural wells in the landscape, or a nest.

4. Reproduction

When a reptile reaches adulthood, it will begin looking for a partner. When two compatible reptiles meet, they will mate and then normally part ways.

Lizards

Among reptiles, lizards have the highest number
of different species—more than 6,400 of them.

Although each species is unique, lizards typically have
four legs (although some are legless), which they use
for movement, climbing, swimming, and various other
tasks. These animals can be found in a rainbow
of vibrant colors and markings.

Marine Iguana

The marine iguana is a unique species of reptile. It is found only on the Galápagos Islands and is one of the only few lizards that are able to forage in the ocean. It is a herbivore that can dive into the sea in search of food, such as algae and seaweed.

Its stubby snout and sharp teeth gives it the perfect tools for scraping algae off rocks and cutting through seaweed. This iguana has the amazing ability of being able to hold its breath for up to one hour. It can dive more than 60 feet deep to help it reach the algae-covered rocks on the seabed. When it resurfaces, after spending such a long time underwater, it sneezes to get rid of the saltwater from inside its nose.

The marine iguana has an interesting relationship with the mockingbird that also lives on the islands. The mockingbird sings when the marine iguana's main predator, the Galápagos hawk, is on the hunt. The iguana have learned that this bird's song also means danger for it, and when it hears the song, it retreats quickly under rocks and into crevices for safety.

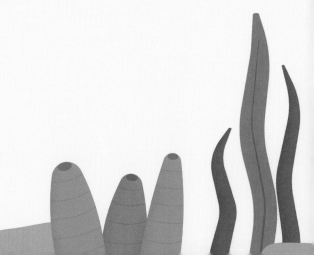

Geckos

Geckos have the largest number of species of any lizard—more than 1,500 different variations. Named after the "gecko" chirping sound that they make, geckos have many unique and interesting characteristics. For example, most gecko species can shed their tails to escape from predators and many have extremely sticky toepads that can adhere to glass. They can also see in exceptional color vision that is more than 350 times better than the human eye.

Madagascan Day Gecko

Although many geckos are nocturnal, the Madagascan day gecko is diurnal (it is active during the day and sleeps at night; the same as us). It is one of the largest daytime geckos, growing up to 8½ inches in length. It likes to spend most of its day climbing in trees, looking for insects and fruit to eat.

Pygmy Gecko

Contrasting with the large Madagascan day gecko, the pygmy gecko is one of the smallest reptiles in the world. It grows to only a little more than ¾ inch long. It is so small that it can easily drown in small pools of water in the rain forest in which it lives. However, the pygmy gecko has developed special skills that are handy for this environment. For example, its skin is water repellent. This, combined with its miniature size, means that it doesn't break the surface of the water when it walks across it.

$\longleftarrow$ ¾ in. $\longrightarrow$

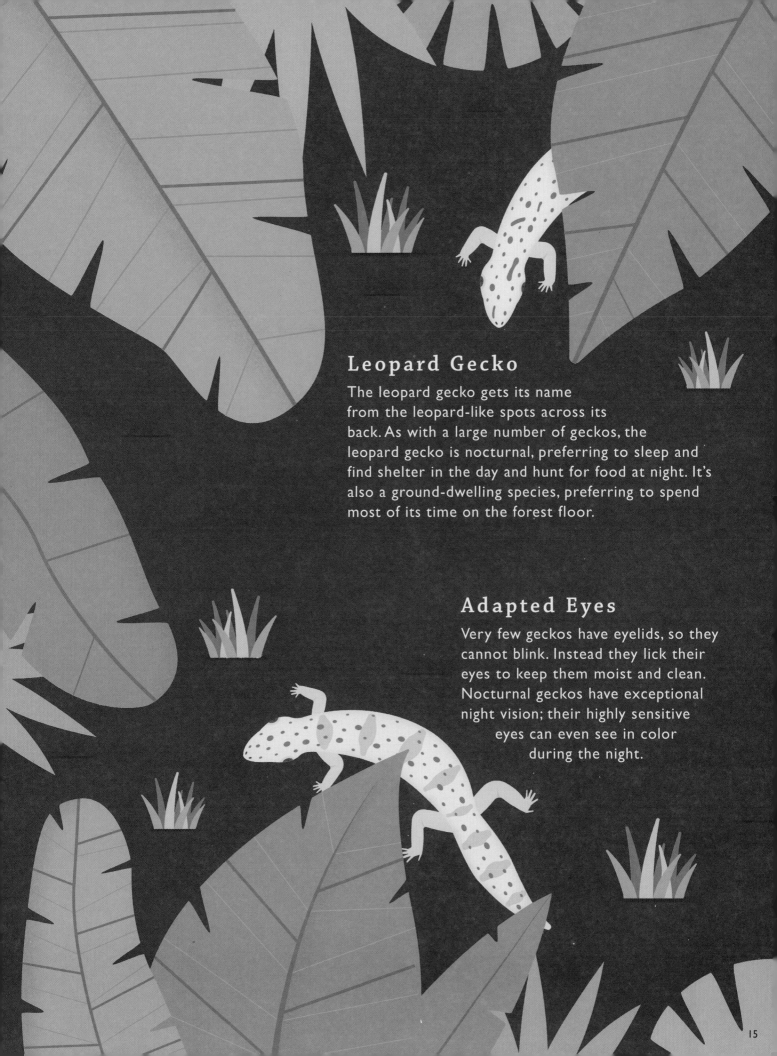

Leopard Gecko

The leopard gecko gets its name from the leopard-like spots across its back. As with a large number of geckos, the leopard gecko is nocturnal, preferring to sleep and find shelter in the day and hunt for food at night. It's also a ground-dwelling species, preferring to spend most of its time on the forest floor.

Adapted Eyes

Very few geckos have eyelids, so they cannot blink. Instead they lick their eyes to keep them moist and clean. Nocturnal geckos have exceptional night vision; their highly sensitive eyes can even see in color during the night.

Draco Lizard

The draco lizard is also known as the gliding lizard, due to its incredible ability to glide through the trees. It does this by extending its unique ribs, which stretch excess skin (usually found hanging on its sides) into winglike shapes. It then jumps out of the trees and begins to glide. While in the air, the draco lizard stabilizes itself using a flap of skin on its lower neck, as well as angles its body and tail to help it steer. There are several reasons this lizard has developed this ability. First, the forest floor contains dangerous predators that would love to have the draco lizard for lunch. By gliding between trees, the draco lizard can minimize its time spent on the ground. Second, the lizard can use its gliding ability to hunt for food and to attract mates. So, if you ever find yourself in the jungles of Southeast Asia, make sure to look up.

Komodo Dragon

Living in Indonesia, the Komodo dragon is the largest species of lizard in the world, reaching up to 10 feet long. It is a dangerous predator, with a long whipping tail and powerful jaws. If this isn't frightening enough, it can also run up to 11 miles per hour in short sprints. It was previously thought that its saliva held toxic bacteria, but it was recently discovered that it's actually venom—another deadly weapon in its arsenal. The Komodo dragon often hunts in packs, so as a group they can take down much larger animals than themselves, such as buffalo, by injecting them with venom in their bites. They are known to also have attacked humans.

Gila Monster

The Gila monster—named after the Arizona Gila River Basin, where it was discovered—is another of the few venomous lizards in the world. It is much smaller than the Komodo dragon, growing only to 2 feet long. Also, unlike the Komodo dragon, it is slow moving and shy in nature, meaning that it probably won't come into contact with any humans. When hunting, the Gila monster bites its prey and then releases venom into the bite through grooves in its teeth (different to a snake, which injects venom through its fangs). This reptile loves to feed on eggs, which are abundant, rich and easy prey. Nowadays, you can still find it in the southwestern United States and northwestern Mexico.

Chameleons

There are more than 200 different species of chameleons, with almost half of them living in one place—the island of Madagascar. They are a particularly interesting species of reptile with many unique tricks and unusual skills for catching prey and avoiding predators.

Panther Chameleon

The panther chameleon is an excellent hunter because it can move silently through the trees using its specially developed limbs to grip the branches. As with most chameleons, the panther chameleon has nearly 360-degree vision. It can move its eyes independently of one another to look for prey or predators coming from all sides.

Jackson's Chameleon

The three horns found on a male Jackson's chameleon gives it a distinct and unique look. It use these horns mainly to attract mates, to fight other males to win mates and to make itself look impressive and dangerous to scare off potential predators. However, it will also use these horns in a defensive manner if it needs to.

Veiled Chameleon

The veiled chameleon, along with many others, uses its long prehensile tail to help it cling to the branches high in the trees. "Prehensile" means that the tail is able to be moved independently and used for grasping.

Tongue Missiles

The tongue of a chameleon is a highly specialized muscle, with a sticky, cuplike tip. When hunting, a chameleon shoots its tongue toward its prey, taking as little as 0.07 second from leaving its mouth to hitting its lunch. A chameleon's tongue can reach one-and-a-half to two times its body length.

Mimicking Movement

For anyone who has seen a chameleon silently navigate through its treetop home, you might have noticed something strange about the way it moves. A chameleon will do everything it can to make its movement as inconspicuous as possible. It moves slowly, gently lifting each limb and then rocking slightly back and forth before taking its next step. It rocks like this to mimic the leaves of a tree blowing in the wind. This stealthy movement helps it to sneak up on prey and avoid the attention of predators.

Camouflage
or Communication

Most people think that a chameleon changes color to
help camouflage itself from predators or prey. Scientists
now know that it's a little more complicated than that.

Camouflage Coincidence

A chameleon doesn't actually change color
to match its surroundings, but does so for a
variety of other reasons. One reason is for
heat regulation. The chameleon can change
to a dark color to absorb more heat
or to a light color to cool off.

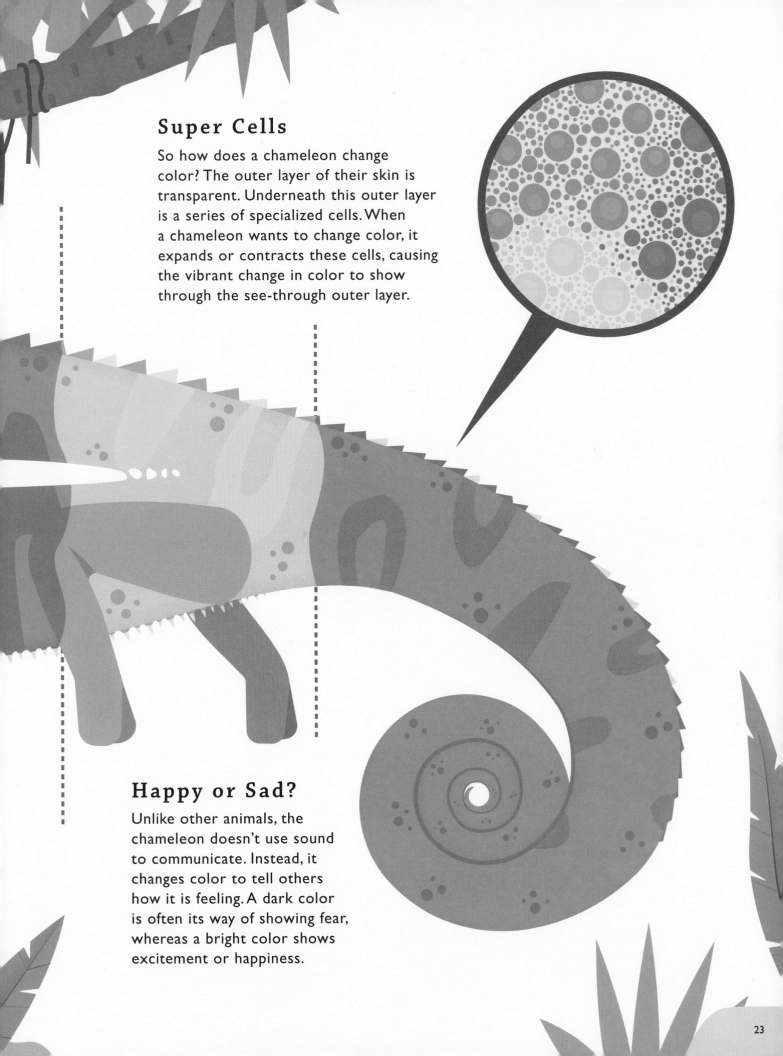

Super Cells

So how does a chameleon change color? The outer layer of their skin is transparent. Underneath this outer layer is a series of specialized cells. When a chameleon wants to change color, it expands or contracts these cells, causing the vibrant change in color to show through the see-through outer layer.

Happy or Sad?

Unlike other animals, the chameleon doesn't use sound to communicate. Instead, it changes color to tell others how it is feeling. A dark color is often its way of showing fear, whereas a bright color shows excitement or happiness.

Thorny Devil Lizard

Despite its fearsome spiny appearance, the Australian thorny devil prefers to use its spikes for defense, not attack. These sharp scales are meant to make the lizard look painful to eat. The thorny devil actually hunts its prey—ants—in a somewhat lazy fashion. It'll find an ant trail, then simply sit and wait for the ants to walk past.

Decoy

If a predator does choose to brave the spikes and threaten to attack the lizard, the thorny devil has one more trick up its sleeve. It will lower its head, tuck it safely between its front legs, and present the attacker with a round decoy head on its back. This keeps the lizard's real head safe if the predator does choose to take a bite.

Not Too Hot, Not Too Cold

The thorny devil will stay in its burrow during the hot summer months and cold winter months, only venturing out when it feels the temperature is just right. This normally occurs during fall and spring. When it does emerge from its burrow, it will change color, depending on the temperature. Just like the chameleon, turning a light color when it is hot helps to deflect the harsh sun, and turning a dark color helps it to absorb more heat during colder periods.

Sailfin Water Lizard

The sailfin water lizard is a large, visually unique reptile that is found only in the Philippines. This 3-foot-long lizard is at home in the trees and streams found in the dense tropical jungles.

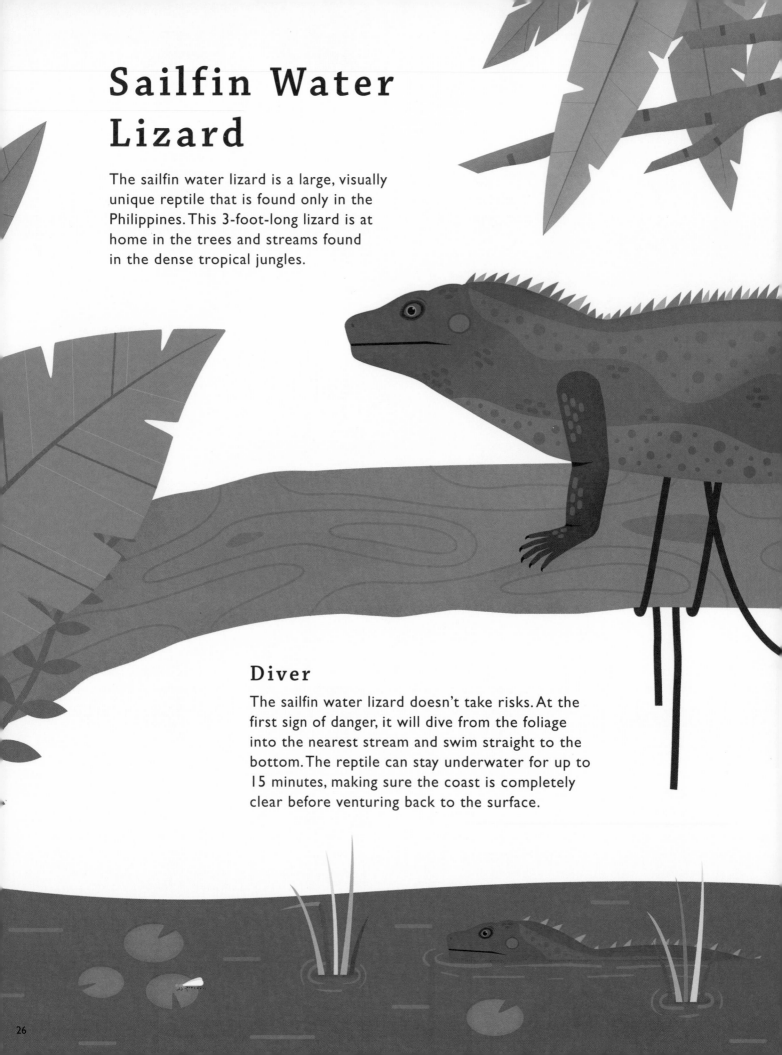

Diver

The sailfin water lizard doesn't take risks. At the first sign of danger, it will dive from the foliage into the nearest stream and swim straight to the bottom. The reptile can stay underwater for up to 15 minutes, making sure the coast is completely clear before venturing back to the surface.

The Sailfin

The most distinguishing feature of this lizard is its large fin. A male will use this 2¾-inch-tall fin to propel itself through water, as well as for territorial displays and heat regulation.

Varying Colors

Sailfin water lizards have been seen in a whole range of colors, such as green, brown, and yellow. When a male gets older, it often turns an interesting shade of blue. This bright color helps the lizard to attract a potential mate.

Skinks

Skinks are a family of lizards with round bodies. Leading skink characteristics include smooth, shiny skin (fish-like), having short or small limbs, snakelike movement, and the ability to detach its tail.

Emerald Tree Skink

The beautifully colored emerald tree skink is believed to be almost completely arboreal, meaning that it spends its entire life living in trees. The emerald tree skink is known to have its own favorite tree, where it can be seen feeding on insects, fruit, and leaves.

Western Three-Toed Skink

Although it may look like a snake, it is actually a skink. The western three-toed skink is known for its tiny front and back legs, each with only three small toes. Therefore, instead of using them to walk, it finds it much easier to move in a snakelike fashion through the undergrowth of the mild forests it inhabits.

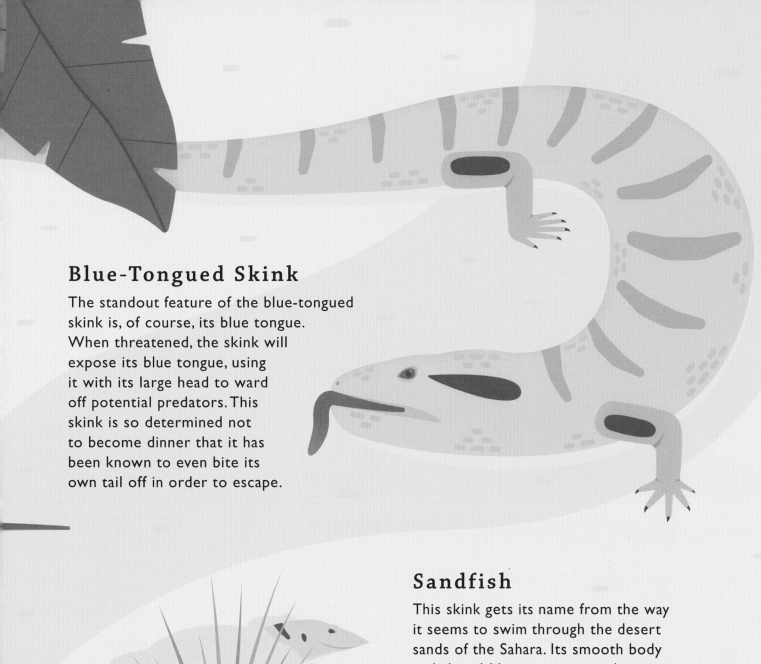

Blue-Tongued Skink

The standout feature of the blue-tongued skink is, of course, its blue tongue. When threatened, the skink will expose its blue tongue, using it with its large head to ward off potential predators. This skink is so determined not to become dinner that it has been known to even bite its own tail off in order to escape.

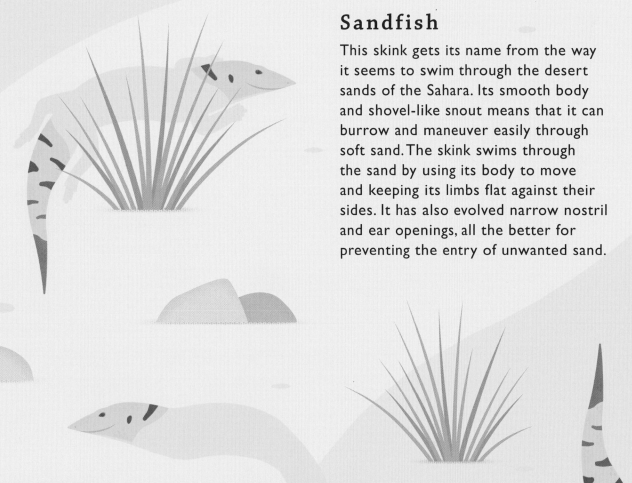

Sandfish

This skink gets its name from the way it seems to swim through the desert sands of the Sahara. Its smooth body and shovel-like snout means that it can burrow and maneuver easily through soft sand. The skink swims through the sand by using its body to move and keeping its limbs flat against their sides. It has also evolved narrow nostril and ear openings, all the better for preventing the entry of unwanted sand.

Extraordinary Lizards

Reptiles have evolved some truly unique and innovative methods for surviving within their harsh environments, and of these, there are none more unique than lizards. Let us take a look at some of the weirdest, most specialized, and well-adapted survival superstars of the lizard world.

Armadillo Girdled Lizard

This spiny, hard-scale lizard gets its name from the mammalian armadillo, because they both share the ability to roll themselves into a defensive ball. The armadillo lizard will use its mouth to grab onto its tail, tucking its limbs inside and leaving only the hard spikey scales exposed.

Basilisk Lizard

No, it's not magic, but the basilisk lizard does have one of the most unbelievable adaptations for escaping predators. At the first sign of danger, it can drop from the trees into a nearby stream and "run" across the surface of the water. It achieves this by maintaining a high speed and by using its long toes to increase the surface area that touches the water.

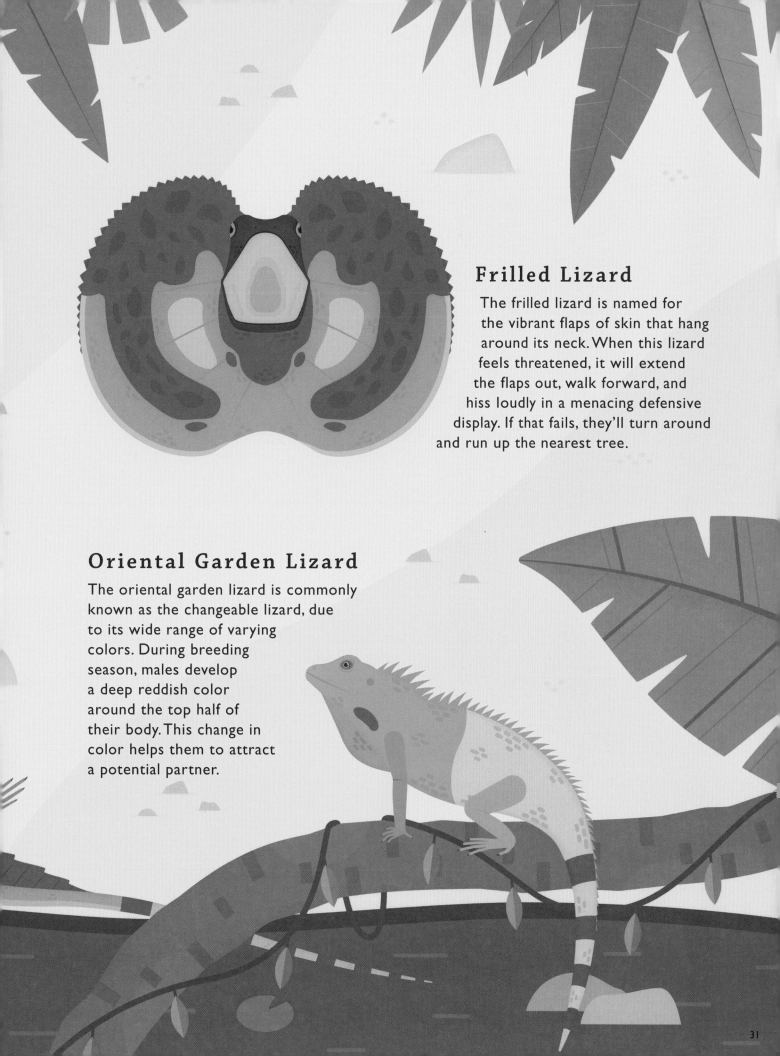

Frilled Lizard

The frilled lizard is named for the vibrant flaps of skin that hang around its neck. When this lizard feels threatened, it will extend the flaps out, walk forward, and hiss loudly in a menacing defensive display. If that fails, they'll turn around and run up the nearest tree.

Oriental Garden Lizard

The oriental garden lizard is commonly known as the changeable lizard, due to its wide range of varying colors. During breeding season, males develop a deep reddish color around the top half of their body. This change in color helps them to attract a potential partner.

Red-Eyed Crocodile Skink

The red-eyed crocodile skink's name comes from a mixture of features found on the lizard. This skink has red rings circling its eyes and rough crocodilian scales.

Distress calls

The skink has a special skill in the lizard world—the ability to make noises. When it feels threatened, it will share its distress with high-pitched whining squeaks.

Rain Forest Home

The red-eyed crocodile skink is a relatively small lizard, measuring on average 6¼ to 8 inches. However, despite its small size, it has a proportionally large, well-armored head for protection. The skink makes its home within plant and tree debris from the tropical rain forests of New Guinea and Indonesia.

Mythical Appearance

The unique appearance of this skink comes not only from its striking red eye markings but also the spiny scales along its back. The red-eyed crocodile skink has four rows of these tapering scales running from its neck to the bottom of its tail. This gives the lizard a dinosaur-like appearance.

Snakes

Snakes are a group of meat-eating reptiles that have replaced walking with slithering. Don't be fooled into thinking their lack of limbs is a disadvantage. Snakes have adapted some incredible ways of catching prey and avoiding predators. Some snakes are venomous, some are immensely strong, and many are masters of disguise. These incredible serpents can be found on every continent except Antarctica. There are more than 3,600 species of snake in the world.

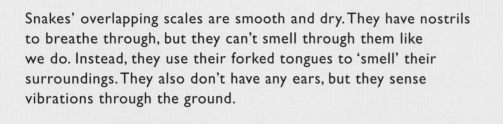

Snakes' overlapping scales are smooth and dry. They have nostrils to breathe through, but they can't smell through them like we do. Instead, they use their forked tongues to 'smell' their surroundings. They also don't have any ears, but they sense vibrations through the ground.

Inland Taipan

The Australian inland taipan is the most venomous snake in the world. One bite from this snake has enough venom to kill more than 100 grown-up men or 250,000 mice.

However, it is a shy and reclusive snake that would much rather slither away and hide than attack a human. Its venom has been specially adapted for hunting mammals, and its main food source is small rodents.

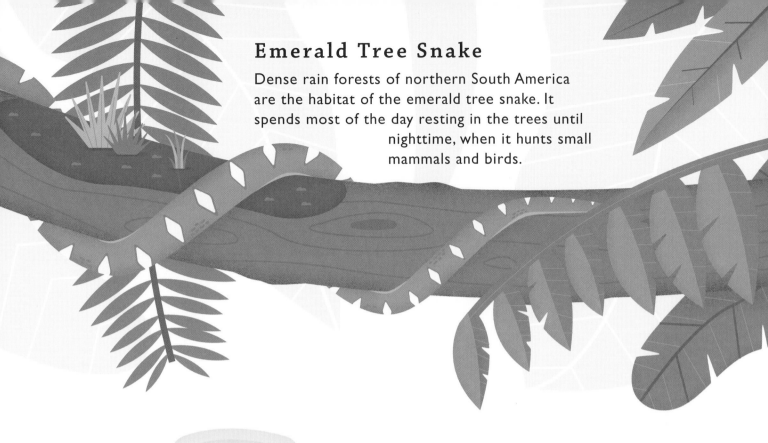

Emerald Tree Snake

Dense rain forests of northern South America are the habitat of the emerald tree snake. It spends most of the day resting in the trees until nighttime, when it hunts small mammals and birds.

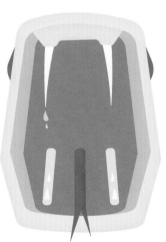

Fangs and Venom

Although most snakes have teeth, venomous snakes have fangs. Fangs are connected to venom sacs in the back of the snake's head. When a snake bites, the venom travels from the sacs to the fangs, which are hollow, so the venom can flow through the fangs and into the prey.

Sea Snake

This is a highly venomous snake found in warm coastal waters from the Indian Ocean to the Pacific. It is specially adapted for life in the water, with a flat tail to help it swim and valves in its nostrils, which close when underwater. Fishermen are the most common people to be bitten, because the snake gets trapped in their nets.

Coral and Milk Snakes

One is deadly, the other is harmless—but which is which?

Friend or Foe?

The rhyme "red to yellow, kill a fellow; red to black, venom lack" is an old saying used to help tell the difference between the deadly coral snake and the harmless milk snake. This refers to the colored bands along both of the snake's bodies.

Milk snake

Unlike the coral snake, the milk snake is completely harmless. The name of the milk snake may suggest that it drinks milk, however, this isn't the case. It feeds on small animals such as rodents and lizards. Due to its lack of venom, the milk snake constricts its prey before swallowing it whole.

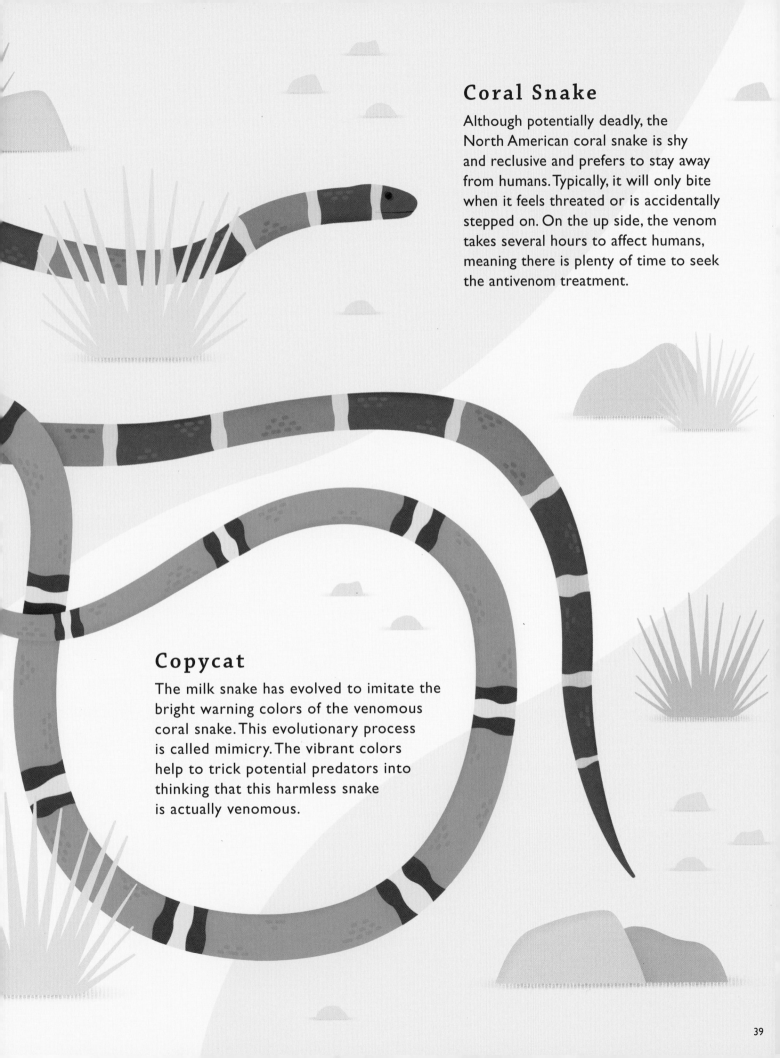

Coral Snake

Although potentially deadly, the North American coral snake is shy and reclusive and prefers to stay away from humans. Typically, it will only bite when it feels threated or is accidentally stepped on. On the up side, the venom takes several hours to affect humans, meaning there is plenty of time to seek the antivenom treatment.

Copycat

The milk snake has evolved to imitate the bright warning colors of the venomous coral snake. This evolutionary process is called mimicry. The vibrant colors help to trick potential predators into thinking that this harmless snake is actually venomous.

Cobras

Cobras are famous for their hooded necks and upright postures. Their venom affects the nervous system of the receiver and, if left untreated, it can be fatal to humans. These incredible snakes have become both worshiped and feared by cultures around the world.

King Cobra

When cornered, the king cobra has a reputation for being one of the most fierce and intimidating snakes on the planet. It is the longest venomous snake, reaching lengths of up to 19 feet. This great length means it could easily look a grown-up human in the eye when in its upright position. The venom it can deliver in one striking bite is enough to kill an elephant.

And if that isn't enough, when in the upright position, it is still able to move forward, emit an angry sharp hiss, and even attack. However, when possible, the king cobra prefers to avoid confrontation, slink away, and hide.

Spitting Cobra

The spitting cobra has developed a terrifying new way to deter potential predators. As its name suggests, the spitting cobra is capable of firing its venom directly out of its fangs toward the threat's face, specifically the eyes. The venom can be accurately shot into a predator's eyes from up to 6 feet 6 inches away, leaving the attacker temporarily blinded.

Ancient Egypt

The Egyptian cobra has a deep and rich history within Egypt. The cobra was used as a symbol for the ancient Egyptian god Wadjet, and this symbol was often used on the crown of the pharaohs (ancient Egyptian kings and queens).

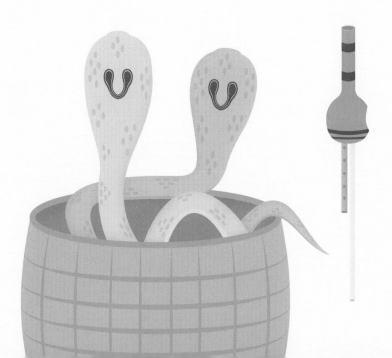

Sound or Sight?

Indian cobras have often been used by street-performing snake charmers. However, the snakes have no external ears, so pay no attention to the music coming from the flute. Instead, the cobras see the shape of the flute as a threat and resort to their upright defensive posture in order to scare it away.

Reticulated Python

Although technically not the biggest snake in the world in terms of weight, the reticulated python is certainly the longest. This giant snake can be found slinking through the damp creeks of Asian rain forests and woodlands.

Reticulated

The name reticulated comes from the repeating pattern that can be found covering these snakes' scales. This pattern helps it to blend into its surroundings, making it easier for it to ambush prey.

How Long?

The reticulated python has been known to grow as long as 24 feet. To put that into perspective, it's around the same length as a small aircraft. The reticulated python is about 2 feet long when it hatches. It grows rapidly during its first two to three years of life, increasing in size sometimes by the height of a grown-up human each year.

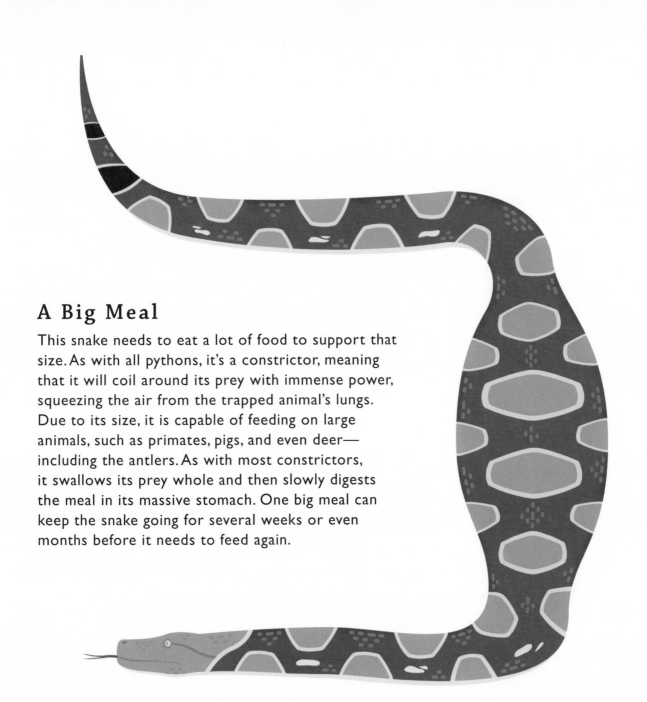

A Big Meal

This snake needs to eat a lot of food to support that size. As with all pythons, it's a constrictor, meaning that it will coil around its prey with immense power, squeezing the air from the trapped animal's lungs. Due to its size, it is capable of feeding on large animals, such as primates, pigs, and even deer—including the antlers. As with most constrictors, it swallows its prey whole and then slowly digests the meal in its massive stomach. One big meal can keep the snake going for several weeks or even months before it needs to feed again.

Egg-Eating Snake

Although there are several species of snakes that eat bird eggs, the egg-eating snake is unique because it will eat nothing else. The egg-eating snake will consume a range of bird eggs, but its favorite is that of the weaverbird. The weaverbird makes elaborate hanging nests for its eggs. This nest is left undefended when the weaverbird ventures off to find food or extra building materials for its nest. The egg-eating snake will take advantage of this, swooping in to swallow the eggs.

Every part of this snake's body has adapted to this hard-to-swallow diet. Like other snakes, the egg-eating snake has an incredibly flexible jaw that can stretch around an egg even larger than its own head. The egg is swallowed whole, cracking only when it reaches a series of ridges along the spine. Once the contents of the egg have been digested, the snake will then regurgitate the leftover broken shell.

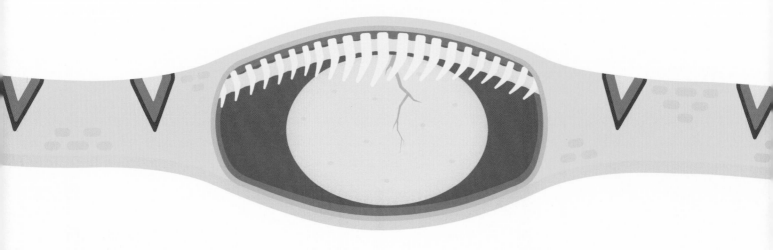

Vipers

Vipers are a type of venomous snake, categorized by large hinged fangs that can fold flat against the roof of their mouths. They typically have broad heads and thick bodies. These snakes are also some of the most versatile snakes in the world. They are found nearly all over the world, live on the ground and in the trees, and can reproduce by eggs and by live-birth.

Horned Viper

The desert-dwelling horned viper gets its name from two hornlike scales above its eyes. As menacing as these horns look, they aren't actually used for attacking. Instead, they protect the snake's eyes from sand.

The horned viper wriggles from side to side to bury itself in the stony desert sand. While half-submerged, it can cool off from the harsh desert sun, hide from predators, and ambush its unsuspecting prey.

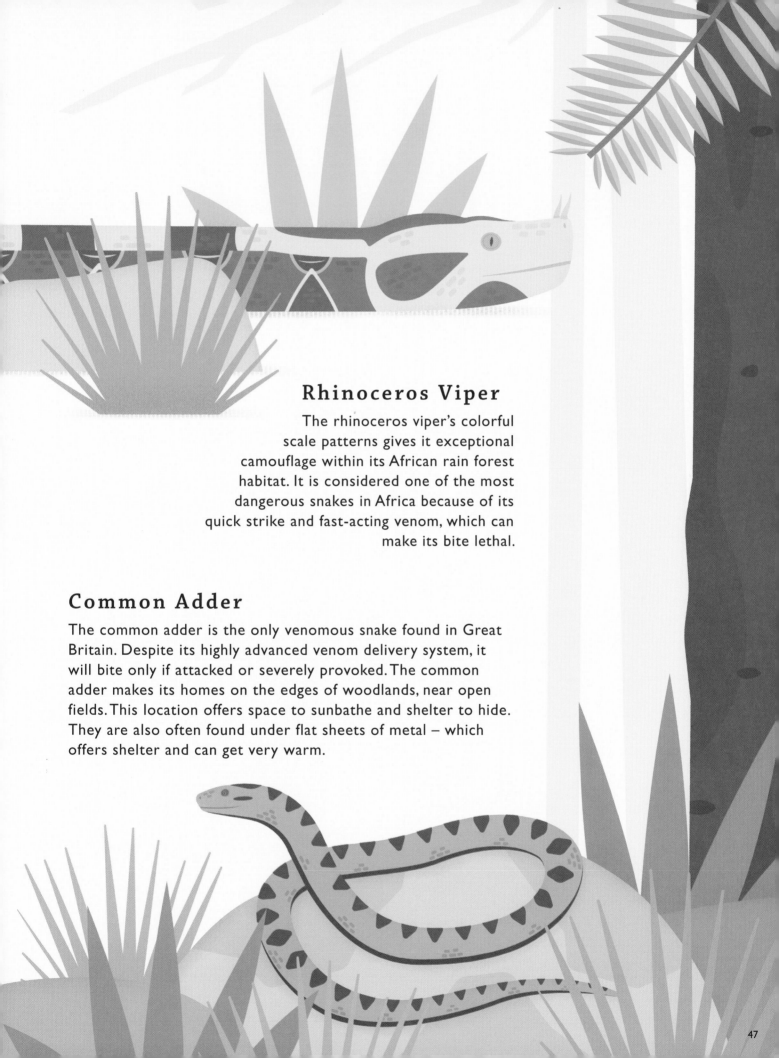

Rhinoceros Viper

The rhinoceros viper's colorful scale patterns gives it exceptional camouflage within its African rain forest habitat. It is considered one of the most dangerous snakes in Africa because of its quick strike and fast-acting venom, which can make its bite lethal.

Common Adder

The common adder is the only venomous snake found in Great Britain. Despite its highly advanced venom delivery system, it will bite only if attacked or severely provoked. The common adder makes its homes on the edges of woodlands, near open fields. This location offers space to sunbathe and shelter to hide. They are also often found under flat sheets of metal – which offers shelter and can get very warm.

Giant Anaconda

The giant anaconda is the largest, heaviest snake in the world. Although its relative the reticulated python is slightly longer, the giant anaconda is far thicker, making it nearly twice as heavy as the python.

Appetite

Such a big snake has a big appetite. The giant anaconda is a nonvenomous constrictor, which means it wraps its massive body around its prey and crushes it to death. It will then swallow its prey whole. It can be a pig, deer, caiman, or even a jaguar. A big meal can keep the snake nourished for several weeks or months.

Swamps

Due to its size, the
giant anaconda can
be cumbersome on
land. For this reason,
it prefers to bathe in
swamps and slow-moving
streams, nearly completely
submerged. These watery
spots can also be perfect
hiding places from which
to ambush its prey.

Worm snake

The name of the worm snake comes from its wormlike appearance and behavior. It spends almost all of its life buried underground, only surfacing at night during warm months.

Deciduous Forests

A worm snake's habitat usually consists of damp, deciduous forests and woodlands. During dryer periods, it seeks out damp soil deeper underground, as it depends on humidity to survive. Deciduous trees shed their leaves during the colder months.

A Rare Sight

On the rare occasion that this snake does venture above ground, it will probably be found hiding inside rotting logs or under rocks and leaves. When above ground, it tries to keep hidden at all times, otherwise it would make an easy meal for a whole range of predators.

Prey

Although it might look like an earthworm and behaves similar to it, the worm snake's main prey is the earthworm. When it catches a worm, it will swallow it alive and whole. If it can't find an earthworm, it may resort to the occasional soft insect or slug.

To the Point

A worm snake will almost never bite an attacker. Instead, it will first try to wriggle away and burrow into the ground. If this fails, it will press the sharp point of its tail into the predator.

Scales

All reptiles have scales. Reptile scales have some unique functions and adaptations that are different from human skin.

Nails or Scales

Reptile scales are made from a tough material called keratin (the same as human hair or fingernails). These keratin scales help protect the reptiles from sharp objects, such as branches or stones, as well as act as a waterproof protective barrier.

Specialized Scales

Many reptiles have scales that have specially adapted to suit their environment. Some geckos have developed toe pads that give them incredible grip while climbing. They can even hang upside down just from the stickiness of these scales. On the other hand, snakes have developed smooth, wide plate scales on their underbelly. These help them to move through rough terrain.

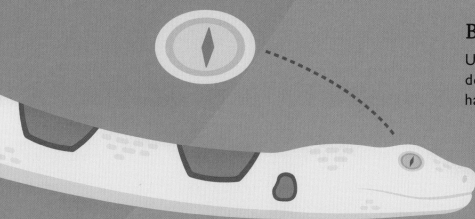

Brille

Unlike humans, many reptiles don't have eyelids. Instead, they have a transparent scale called *brille*. Without brille, reptilian eyes would be much more susceptible to being damaged or infected.

Slimy Scales

Contrary to popular belief, snake scales aren't slimy. Snakes have interlocking scales that create a soft, smooth texture. They are specifically designed to keep moisture inside the body. This helps them to retain the vital water they need in hot desert climates.

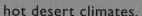

Molting

Most reptiles shed their skin to get rid of old dead scales and parasites. Lizards and other reptiles usually shed their skin gradually, in small pieces over time. In contrast, snakes periodically shed their entire skin all at once, leaving behind a long snake-shaped tube.

Turtles and Tortoises

Most turtles and tortoises are easily recognizable by the large domelike shell across their backs. Although it is made from the same material (keratin) as human hair, the shell doesn't lack sense. It has a full web of nerve endings running through it, meaning the turtle or tortoise can feel every inch of shell. Turtles spend almost their entire lives in the water, whereas most tortoises can't even swim. These mostly gentle armored reptiles are some of the longest living and resilient reptiles on the planet. There are only 350 known species of turtles and tortoises.

Tortoise

The tortoise is actually classed as a land-dwelling turtle. Unlike most other turtles, however, a tortoise usually can't swim and is normally a herbivore, meaning it only eats plants.

Marathon Winner

Although the tortoise isn't famous for its speed, slow and steady may win the race. Even with its size it has no trouble traveling huge distances every day.

Defensive Shell

The tortoise has the amazing defensive ability of retreating its head and limbs back inside its shells when it is threatened. The rock-hard shell makes it incredibly difficult for any potential predators to make a meal out of the soft tortoise inside.

Exo and Endo

Unlike most animals who have either an exoskeleton (skeleton on the outside) or endoskeleton (skeleton inside the body), the tortoise has both. The internal bones include leg bones, a rib cage, and a spine, with the shell forming an external skeleton.

Life story

Tortoise shells are made from keratin, which is also found in your fingernails. The shell can tell you a lot about the tortoise inside. Similar to a tree trunk, the rings on the shell can help determine the age of the tortoise. A light shell color tells you the tortoise originates from a hot climate.

Giant Tortoise

"Giant tortoise" refers to the large size of these animals, and the term covers two groups and many species of tortoise. One group is the Galapagos tortoises; the other is the Seychelles giant tortoises. These are some of the oldest living animals on the planet; one giant tortoise has been recorded as living for 152 years. The stereotype of the slow-moving, chilled-out tortoise really fits the giant tortoise, because it can spend about 16 hours a day sleeping. The rest of the time it spends grazing on grass and cacti. It also has the impressive ability to go without food or water for a whole year if it needs to, because it can store some of what it consumes for emergencies.

Although this reptile might be well adapted to surviving in the wild, it has, unfortunately, become endangered due to human interference and food competition with farm animals. There are only 15,000 left in the wild, but the Galapagos species group has been placed under strict protection of the Ecuadorian government, which will hopefully help numbers to increase.

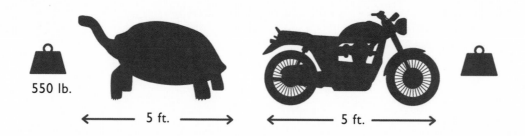

550 lb.   ← 5 ft. →   ← 5 ft. →

Weighing up to 550 pounds and growing to more than 5 feet in length,
its size and weight is easily comparable to those of an average motorcycle
(but a motorcycle would certainly get you from A to B much quicker).

Leatherback Turtle

The leatherback turtle is the largest of all turtles. It gets its name from the soft, rubbery shell that sweeps across its back. Most turtles have a stiff, bony shell, but the leatherback's shell is much more flexible.

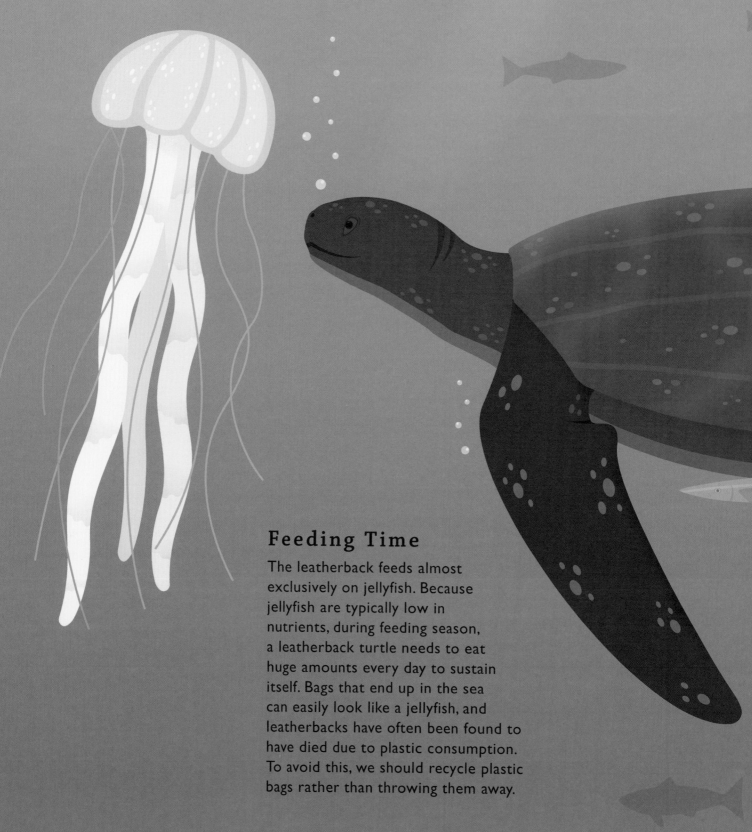

Feeding Time

The leatherback feeds almost exclusively on jellyfish. Because jellyfish are typically low in nutrients, during feeding season, a leatherback turtle needs to eat huge amounts every day to sustain itself. Bags that end up in the sea can easily look like a jellyfish, and leatherbacks have often been found to have died due to plastic consumption. To avoid this, we should recycle plastic bags rather than throwing them away.

Far and Wide

The leatherback turtle has the ability to swim great distances. Ridges on its shell help the turtle to conserve energy on its huge migrations, which can sometimes be more than 4,000 miles.

Friendly Followers

Remora fish (or suckerfish) can often be seen swimming alongside a leatherback turtle. The fish and turtle have a relationship that helps both of them. The remora fish helps the turtle by eating any dead skin, algae, or parasites that have become attached to the turtle, and in exchange it gets a free meal.

Turtle hatchlings

Turtles return to the beach of their own hatching to lay their eggs. This decision guarantees the hatchlings the best chance of survival.

Turtle Boil

Almost all infant turtles on the same beach hatch at the exact same time. The sight of thousands of baby turtles emerging from their nests in unison has led to the term "turtle boil," which compares the sight to that of a pot of boiling water.

Safety in Numbers

There is an evolutionary reason the turtles all hatch at the same time. The journey from the nest to the sea is the most dangerous time in a turtle's life. The immense number of turtles heading toward the sea helps to overwhelm any would-be predators, giving the turtles the best chance of survival.

Giant Nests

The mother turtle will tirelessly dig her nest for up to 3 hours. When she is satisfied with it, she will lay up to 200 eggs. Interestingly, the temperature of the sand will determine the gender of these baby turtles. A cool temperature will produce more males, and a warm one will lead to more females.

Swimming Frenzy

The lucky hatchlings that make it to the sea will start what is known as a "swimming frenzy." This is when the young turtles swim as hard as they can to get away from the predator-infested shores and out to safer waters.

Green Sea Turtle

The green sea turtle is one of the seven different species of sea turtle, all of which are endangered. The green sea turtle gets its name from the color on the tops of its flippers and head.

Up for Air

The green sea turtle is a reptile, so it breathes oxygen just like us. Unlike fish, a turtle doesn't have gills to filter oxygen from the water. Instead, it must come to the surface and take a deep breath before diving back down.

Egg-cellent Memory

A female green sea turtle will migrate long distances from its feeding grounds to a sandy beach so it can lay its eggs. The incredible thing is that the beach it chooses is often the very same beach on which she hatched more than 10 years earlier.

Vegetarian

A grown-up green sea turtle eats mainly plants. It will eat a whole range of underwater vegetables, such as seaweed, sea grass, and algae. In contrast to an adult, a newly hatched green sea turtle is an omnivore, meaning it eats both plants and animals, and it will happily eat small crabs and jellyfish.

Sunny Seas

The green sea turtle spends its life swimming through tropical and subtropical seas. As with all reptiles, the green sea turtle is cold blooded and need the sun's rays to warm up. It usually does this by swimming close to the surface of the water or occasionally by sunbathing on land.

Common Snapping Turtle

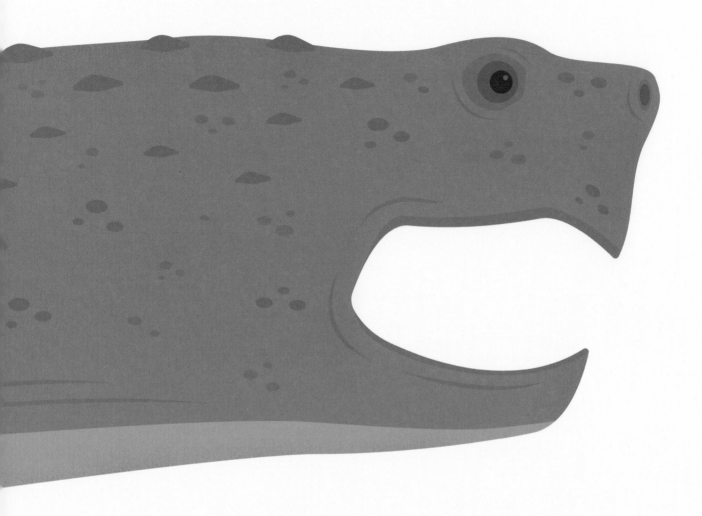

The common snapping turtle is a species of freshwater turtle. It spends most of its days buried in the sediment of slow-moving rivers or resting at the bottom of deeper ponds and lakes. This turtle is an omnivore, meaning it eats both animals and vegetation. What it eats depends on the food sources available to it at the time. This can include insects, fish, frogs, small mammals, and a whole range of underwater greens. The snapping turtle can behave very differently, depending on where it is. For example, if you encountered one while in the water, it would probably swim away and hide. However, when confronted out of the water, it can be much more aggressive and dangerous. It has a powerful bite and a sharp, beaklike snout that you certainly wouldn't want to get your fingers caught in.

Crocodiles and Alligators

Crocodiles and alligators are members of the reptile order of crocodilia. This order contains some of the largest and most dangerous reptiles in the world. These thick-scaled creatures have long powerful tails, making them excellent swimmers and therefore fierce hunters. Crocodilia predate the dinosaurs. It's no wonder they have become some of the most infamous reptiles today. Only 24 species are known and no new species have been discovered for over 100 years.

Saltwater Crocodile

The saltwater crocodile is the world's largest living reptile. It can grow between 16 and 23 feet in length—that's longer than some cars. The saltwater crocodile—or "saltie" as it is called affectionately in Australia—can be found in many places off the western Pacific and eastern Indian oceans, predominantly in eastern India, Southeast Asia, and northern Australia. This makes it the most widely distributed crocodile species in the world. Its habitats include swamps, marshes, and river mouths, but it has been known to use its excellent swimming abilities to swim out to sea.

This crocodile will eat pretty much anything its jaws can fit around, but its normal diet includes water buffalo, cattle, crabs, turtles, and many other unlucky mammals. Although it has powerful jaws, the crocodile can also use them to gently scoop up infant crocodiles in its mouth and safely transport them from one place to another.

Bizarrely, the crocodile swallows stones on purpose. This may seem strange, but these stones help to grind up food in its stomach and also help it to sink in the water.

Saltwater Monster

The saltwater crocodile may be the most dangerous reptile on the planet. It is highly aggressive toward anything that enters its territory, and it is capable of launching a vicious attack from the water.

Record Holder

Not only does the saltwater crocodile hold the record for being the largest reptile, but it also has a scarier achievement. A saltwater crocodile has produced the most powerful bite ever recorded by an animal at 3,700 psi (units of pressure). To illustrate just how powerful that is, us humans have an average bite of 270 psi, and lions and tigers are able to produce a crushing 1,000 psi of force. This means that the saltie's bite is nearly four times stronger than that of a lion. Such incredible power means that it would be virtually impossible to escape from its massive tooth-filled jaws.

Crocodile Tears

The term "crocodile tears" is often used to refer to someone who is displaying false sadness or emotion. Crocodiles and alligators are known to produce liquid from their eyes while feeding. Although scientists aren't completely sure why this occurs, they do know it's not sadness.

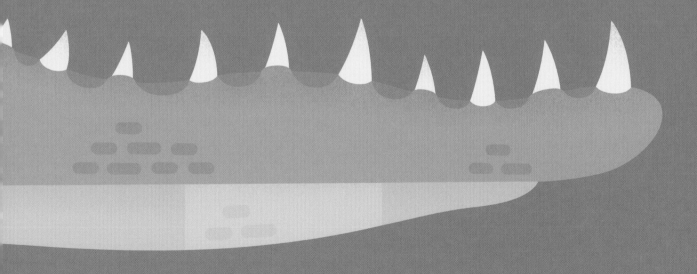

Freshwater Crocodile

Unlike the larger saltwater crocodile, the freshwater crocodile is a smaller crocodilian species, averaging about 10 feet long. As its name suggests, the freshwater crocodile prefers to live in freshwater rivers and creeks in the north of Australia.

Fancy a Swim?

The freshwater crocodile is much less aggressive toward humans than its saltwater relative, despite having the sharper teeth. It tends to attack only if it feels cornered or threatened. It is even considered safe to swim with a freshwater crocodile—if you're brave enough.

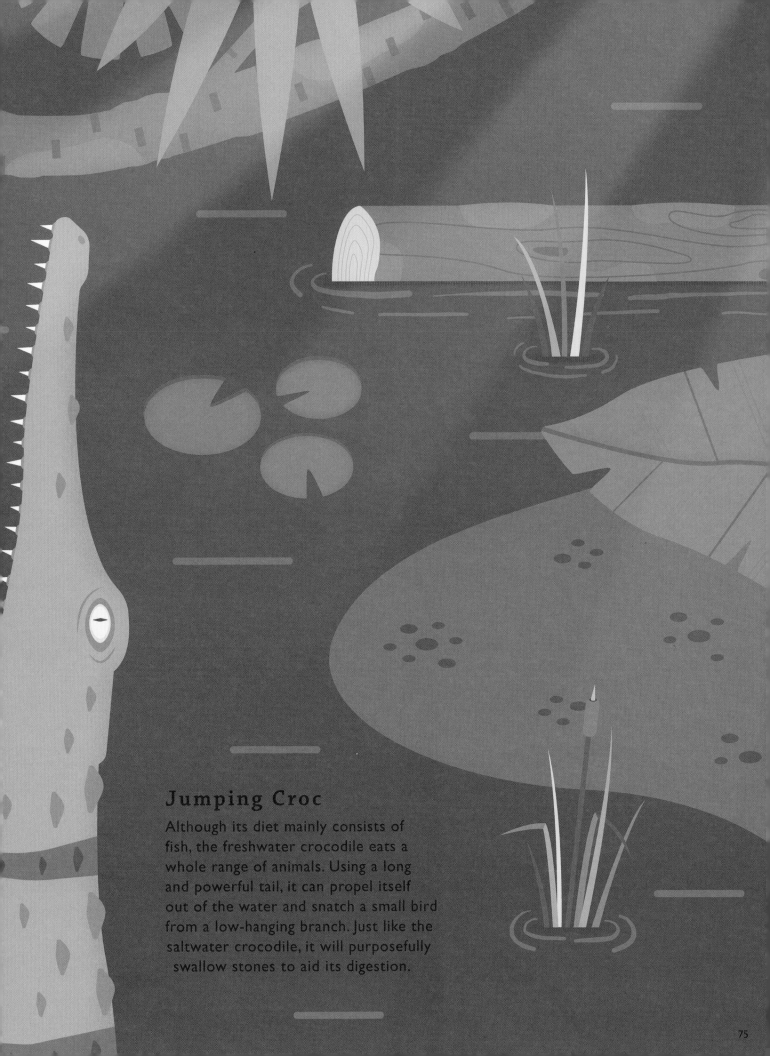

Jumping Croc

Although its diet mainly consists of fish, the freshwater crocodile eats a whole range of animals. Using a long and powerful tail, it can propel itself out of the water and snatch a small bird from a low-hanging branch. Just like the saltwater crocodile, it will purposefully swallow stones to aid its digestion.

Gharial Crocodile

This strange-looking crocodile is the gharial, sometimes known as the fish-eating crocodile. The gharial's body has adapted to give it a superior fish-catching advantage over most other crocodile species. It has an extremely specialized nose that can sense movement within the water. It rapidly shakes its head from side to side, which helps it to judge exactly where its fishy meal is located. Using its slender jaws (the narrowest of any crocodile despite its large size), it grabs the fish. Its jaws are filled with more than 100 razor-sharp teeth, perfect for gripping and holding onto its slippery prey. The male gharial uses the lump on its snout, called a ghara (the Indian word for "pot"), to blow bubbles in the water in order to attract a mate. Using the ghara, it can also make sounds to show off to potential partners. It is so well adapted to its watery home that it will only drag itself onto the riverbank to bask in the sun or to nest.

Chinese Alligator

The Chinese alligator is smaller than its American cousin, growing on average to 5 feet compared to the American alligator's giant 10- to 13-foot length.

This is the only species of alligator to live outside the Americas, and it dwells only in a specific area within China. The Chinese alligator makes its home in the lower section of the Chang River, preferring the slow-moving, calm waters. Its diet consists mainly of fish. However, if fish are in short supply, it will resort to a small bird or rodent.

The Chinese alligator will dig extensive tunnels and burrows with several chambers and sections. It uses these tunnels to hide from potential predators and also for warmth during the cool months of the year.

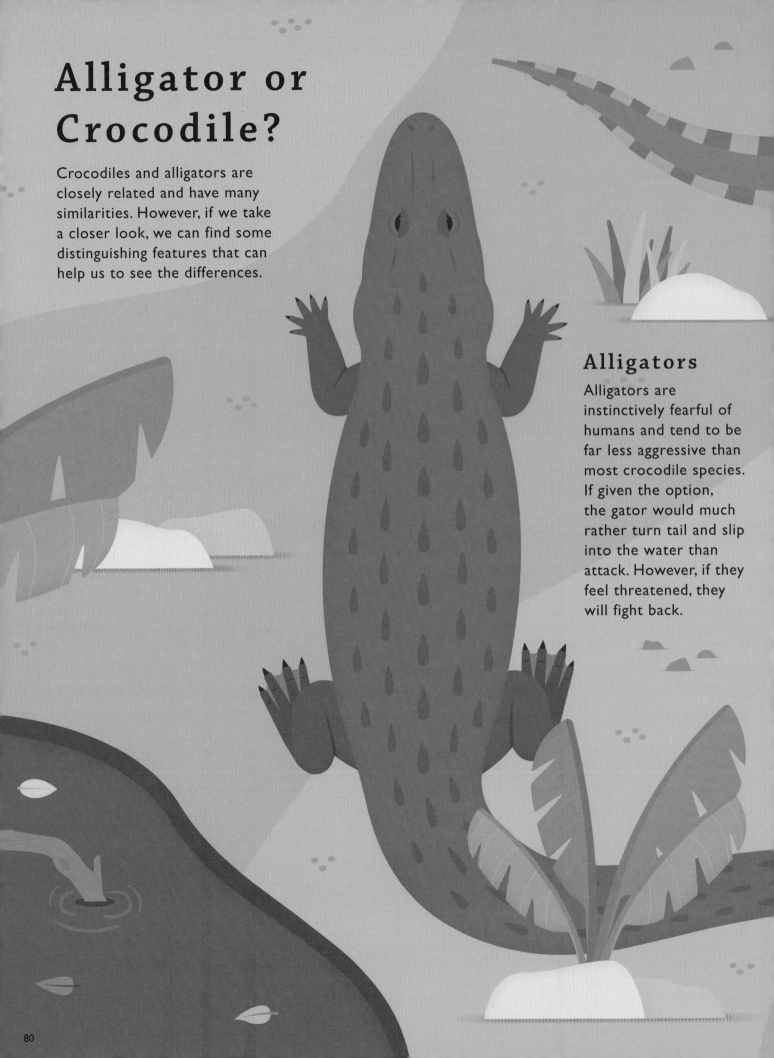

Alligator or Crocodile?

Crocodiles and alligators are closely related and have many similarities. However, if we take a closer look, we can find some distinguishing features that can help us to see the differences.

Alligators

Alligators are instinctively fearful of humans and tend to be far less aggressive than most crocodile species. If given the option, the gator would much rather turn tail and slip into the water than attack. However, if they feel threatened, they will fight back.

Crocodile species can vary greatly in size, from the smallest dwarf crocodile measuring only 5 feet to the giant saltwater crocodile growing up to 23 feet.

Crocodiles

Perhaps not the safest way to tell the difference, but if you can see any bottom teeth when the mouth is closed, then you're looking at a crocodile.

An easier way to tell the difference at a distance is to look at the color of the crocs and gators. Alligators typically have a much darker grayish tone to their skin, but crocodiles usually have a greenish hue.

Habitats
and Environments

Because reptiles can be found on every continent except Antarctica, they live in countless habitats and environments. Journey through this section to find out about the reptiles that live within blistering deserts, soaked rain forests, and more. Discover the environmental challenges and habitat damage caused by humans—and what we can do to help save their world.

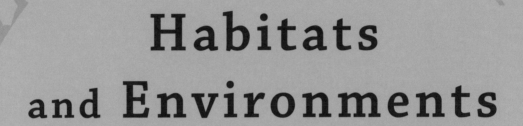

Deserts

Some of the harshest and most extreme environments on the planet are found in deserts. With daytime temperatures averaging a blistering 100 degrees Fahrenheit and cold nights plummeting down to 25 degrees Fahrenheit, the reptiles that live in them have developed some incredible methods of survival.

Leopard Lizard

This lizard gets its name from the distinct leopardlike spot markings on its back. It is a skilled predator and will lay in waiting to ambush its prey (insects and small mammals). It can also run fast for its size, using only its hind feet, which means that many prey that slip past the ambush can be chased and caught.

Desert Tortoise

The desert tortoise has adapted to life in the blistering daytime heat and nighttime cold of the Mojave Desert. To do this, it digs burrows, where it takes shelter from the harsh temperature extremes. At least 95 percent of its life will be spent in burrows.

Mojave Rattlesnake

A highly venomous native of the Mojave Desert, this rattlesnake likes to hide in grassy and rocky areas. You would hear this snake before you see it, because it shakes its tail to make the distinct rattling sound, warning predators to stay away. Another less-known warning signal of the Mojave rattlesnake is that it hisses like a cat when threatened.

Common Collared Lizard

The common collared lizard is so-named because it has bands of black around its neck and shoulders, which looks like a collar. This lizard has the ability to run on its back legs, making it look like a miniature theropod dinosaur.

Dry Desert

The Mojave Desert is home to a place called Death Valley. It is called this because it is the driest and hottest place in the whole of North America. It's so dry it gets only about 5 inches of rainfall each year.

Rain Forests

These incredible habitats cover about 6 percent of the earth's surface, but they are home to an abundance of animal and plant life.

Boyd's Forest Dragon

This lizard spends most of its day clinging to tree trunks, waiting for unsuspecting prey to cross its path. This prey usually consists of small insects and worms. Because only a limited amount of sunlight makes it through the dense canopy of the rain forest, this lizard has adapted to no longer need direct sunlight to stay warm. Instead, it lets its body temperature fluctuate with the air temperature.

Boa Constrictor

When hunting for food, the boa constrictor will grab its prey, coil around it, and squeeze with incredible strength before swallowing the victim whole. It is a master of camouflage, and the colors and markings of an individual snake will depend on the environment it is trying to blend into.

Bush Viper

The bush viper is a patient hunter. It will sit and wait, often for long periods of time, for its prey to come into range. However, things speed up once the victim comes within striking range. The viper will then coil and fire its head with lighting speed toward its prey.

Caiman Lizard

The caiman lizard splits its time between swimming, using its specially adapted flat tail to speed through the water, and lounging around on branches and in trees. It is a carnivore (meaning it only eats other animals) and its diet consists mainly of snails and insects plus the occasional small fish and rodent.

Leaf-Tailed gecko

You could easily be forgiven for thinking you were looking at a browning leaf instead of a gecko. Its leaflike appearance and the ability to sit completely still means that would-be predators will often walk straight past it.

Emerald Wonders

Despite their relatively small coverage of the planet, rain forests are home to about 50 percent of the world's diversity of plant and animal species. To be classed as a rain forest, the area must get at least 75 inches of rainfall every year. However, it is often much higher, and most rain forests receive somewhere between 100 and 175 inches of rain each year. This is about the height of 2.2 to 3.5 mailboxes. Not only are rain forests home to a vast range of plants and animals, they also help us. About one-fourth of all modern medicines get their ingredients from rain forest plants.

Mountain Parks

In general, reptiles don't tend to live at high altitudes. This is because they are cold blooded and need the hot sun of warm climates to help warm up. However, there are a few reptiles that have made their homes at higher altitudes, such as the parks that surround mountain ranges.

Western Skink

The western skink can often be found in dry open forests at altitudes of up to 6,900 feet above sea level. It is a hardy species that can adapt to a varying range of environments and habitats. If caught by a predator, the skink can shed its tail, which wriggles even after it's detached, distracting the prey and giving the lizard a chance to escape.

Garter Snake

Commonly found living at altitudes of up to 13,000 feet, the garter snake is exclusively found in North America. It makes its home in the grassland and forest parks that surround American mountain ranges, such as Yosemite and the Sierra Nevada.

Eastern Fence Lizard

The eastern fence lizard has been seen living in the stony woodlands of Rocky Mountain National Park. If you ever encounter this lizard, you may see it doing push-ups. Much as it may look like the lizard is working out, it is actually a form of social communication – expressing strength and status.

Urban Habitats

The newest type of environment found on earth are urban habitats. They present some harsh challenges for the reptiles that choose to brave these concrete jungles. Some species of reptiles have rapidly adapted to live next to humans in homes, offices, and even underground stations.

Common House Gecko

As its name suggests, the common house gecko can often be found climbing on walls, ceilings, and rooftops of buildings in Southeast Asia. They are nocturnal hunters that forage for insects. At nighttime, insects attracted by the city's bright lights in turn attract the geckos for their dinner.

City Snake

The North American brown snake is often locally referred to as a city snake. This has come about because it is the most common snake found in urban environments. Building sites have become one of its favorite places, where there is usually an abundance of wood, rocks, or scrap for it to hide under. Snakes are also often attracted to cities because of the abundance of rats – food!

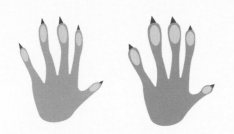

Anole Lizard

The city-dwelling anole lizard has evolved longer limbs and larger scales on the bottom of its toes to help it climb on flat surfaces, such as glass. This adaptation is not found in the anole lizard that lives in the forest. This is why scientists know that it is the urban habitat that has caused this evolution in the city anole. It can often be seen climbing tall glass windows with ease in Puerto Rico, where this discovery was first made.

Mediterranean House Gecko

A nocturnal species, the Mediterranean house gecko thrives in an urban environment due to the abundance of food sources and the low number of predators. It often makes its home inside the walls of local houses, sleeping through the day and emerging to forage at night.

Habitat Loss

Earth is a complex, delicately balanced ecosystem, where even small changes make the difference between survival and extinction for not only reptiles but all animals.

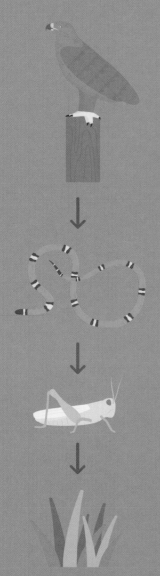

Pollution

Pollution and the dumping of harmful chemicals into reptile habitats have devastating consequences. Because reptiles are much more sensitive than other animals, pollution is particularly dangerous for them. A solution to these concerns would be for companies to reduce their waste products and safely dispose of them.

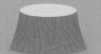

Knock-on Effect

The picture above shows how reptiles form key components within the food chain, both as prey and as predator. If the number of reptiles in a habitat drops, this will have a knock-on effect. A 'chain reaction' can occur if a species becomes extinct – e.g. lack of food or over-population of prey.

Waste and Spills

Another major danger facing the natural world is waste. Oil spills, from both deforestation vehicles and ships, are deadly to reptiles. Reptiles can also confuse litter (such as plastic bags) for prey or a hiding place. If eaten, plastic can be fatal, and if trapped in a bag, the animal can suffocate.

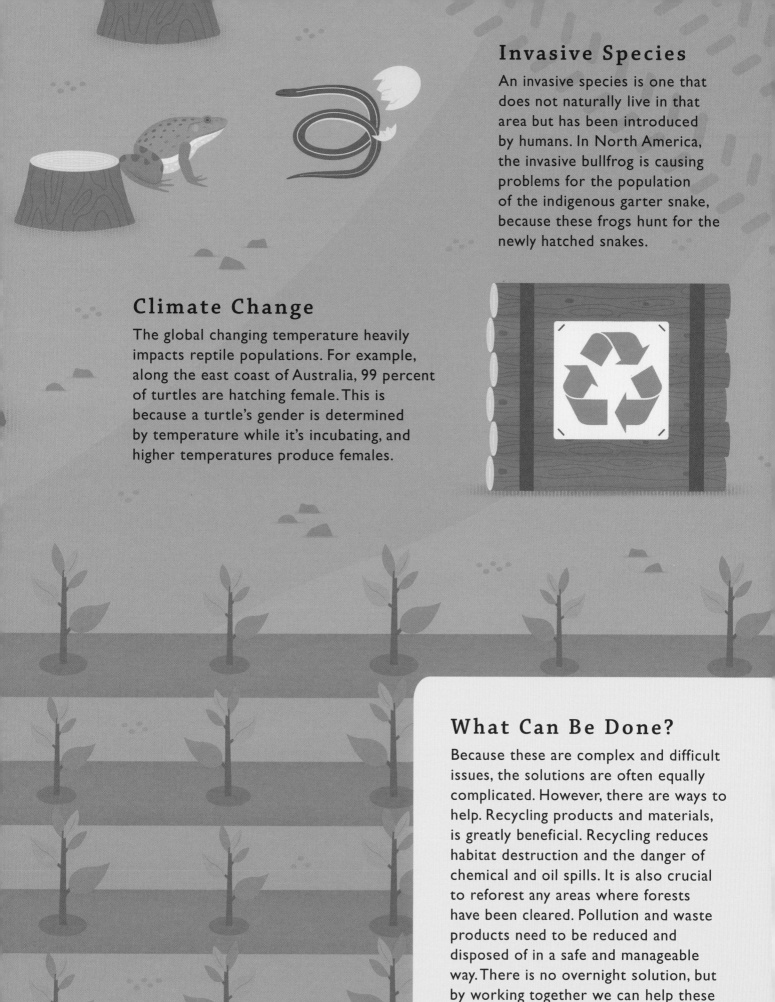

Invasive Species

An invasive species is one that does not naturally live in that area but has been introduced by humans. In North America, the invasive bullfrog is causing problems for the population of the indigenous garter snake, because these frogs hunt for the newly hatched snakes.

Climate Change

The global changing temperature heavily impacts reptile populations. For example, along the east coast of Australia, 99 percent of turtles are hatching female. This is because a turtle's gender is determined by temperature while it's incubating, and higher temperatures produce females.

What Can Be Done?

Because these are complex and difficult issues, the solutions are often equally complicated. However, there are ways to help. Recycling products and materials, is greatly beneficial. Recycling reduces habitat destruction and the danger of chemical and oil spills. It is also crucial to reforest any areas where forests have been cleared. Pollution and waste products need to be reduced and disposed of in a safe and manageable way. There is no overnight solution, but by working together we can help these incredible animals thrive.

Vanishing Reptiles

There are currently around 2000 species of reptile that are listed as either endangered or critically endangered; that's around one in five of all reptile species. Without a change in our attitudes towards the environment, beautiful reptiles such as the hump-nosed lizard (shown above) could become extinct. Because reptiles have evolved to live in some of the more extreme environments on Earth, this also makes them more sensitive to small changes within their habitats. Many reptiles play a key role within the food chain, being both predator and prey. Therefore, the loss of reptile species could have a severe knock-on effect for the rest of their habitat by reducing the food supply for other animals within the habitat. There are many dangers that threaten reptiles and their habitats. One of the biggest problems is climate change, which forces reptiles to retreat in shelters to prevent over-heating.

This means that they miss out on opportunities for feeding and reproducing. Another problem is logging and deforestation, which destroys habitats and leaves reptiles with nowhere to hide, no shelter and no food. This is a particular threat in tropical regions, where a large number of reptiles live. To keep these creatures protected and safe, we need to find alternatives to logging and deforestation. An effective conservation and reforestation plan can help to reduce and repair damage already done to these environments. Using less packaging and recycling waste materials can help, too, because it means that fewer new materials need to be sourced to make things. This is increasingly important to save the habitats of reptiles, some of the most diverse, interesting, and remarkable creatures in the world.

Glossary

Adaptation When animal characteristics, developed through natural selection, help that animal to thrive in its environment and reproduce.

Brille Transparent, immovable scales that cover the eyes of some reptiles, acting like eyelids.

Camouflage To alter appearance and conceal oneself in the environment.

Carnivore An animal with a meat-based diet.

Constrictor A snake that coils around its prey, squeezing and suffocating it.

Decoy Something used to trick or confuse, for example, the false head of the thorny devil.

Diurnal To sleep during the night and be active by day.

Extinction When a species dies out through natural or man-made causes.

Herbivore An animal with a plant-based diet.

Nocturnal To sleep during the day and be active by night.

Omnivore An animal with a diet that includes both plants and meat.

Prehensile Having the ability to move, grasp, and hold; a chameleon's tail is prehensile.

Regurgitate To surge back; to vomit.

Reproduction The natural process by which organisms multiply.

Reticulated Netlike; in regards to the reticulated python, a reference to its pattern.

Theropod A carnivorous type of dinosaur that tended to walk on two legs.

Venom A poisonous fluid produced by some creatures.

Vertebrates Creatures that have a spinal column, or backbone. As well as reptiles, these include humans, other mammals, birds, and amphibians.

1. **Green Sea Turtle** (*Chelonia Mydas*) **Tropical Seas**
2. **Common Collared Lizard** (*Crotaphytus Collaris*) **Mexico/USA**
3. **Giant Tortoise** (*Chelonoidis Nigra*) **Seychelles**
4. **Hump Nosed Lizard** (*Lyriocephalus Scutatus*) **Sri Lanka**
5. **Common House Gecko** (*Hemidactylus Frenatus*) **Southeast Asia**
6. **Oriental Garden Lizard** (*Calotes Versicolour*) **Asia**
7. **Armadillo Lizard** (*Ouroborus Cataphractus*) **South Africa**
8. **Emerald Tree Skink** (*Lamprolepis Smaragdina*) **Asia/Australia**

9. **Mediterranean House Gecko** (*Hemidactylus Turcicus*) **Eu**
10. **Saltwater Crocodile** (*Crocodylus Porosus*) **Asia/Australi**
11. **Mojave Rattlesnake** (*Crotalus Scutulatus*) **USA/Mexico**
12. **Panther Chameleon** (*Furcifer Paradalis*) **Madagascar**
13. **Leaf Tailed Gecko** (*Uroplatus Phantasticus*) **Madagascar**
14. **American Alligator** (*Alligator Mississippiensis*) **USA**
15. **Garter Snake** (*Thamnophis Sirtalis*) **North America**
16. **Frilled Lizard** (*Chlamydosaurus Kingii*) **Australia**